# CONVERSATION BETWEEN THE WIND AND THE SNOW

Contact the Author at:
jaffajuice2005@hotmail.co.uk

Collected Poems 1980 - 2010

Philip Wade

© Philip Wade 2010
First published in 2010 by Philip Wade

Printed by Dalton Printers, Cardiff
www.daltonprinters.co.uk

ISBN 978-0-9566594-0-8

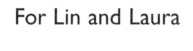

For Lin and Laura

# Contents

| | |
|---|---|
| Silent Places | 5 |
| Conversation Between the Wind and the Snow | 6 |
| Diagnosis | 10 |
| Cold Air | 11 |
| Edelman | 12 |
| Memento Mori | 13 |
| Shadows | 14 |
| Topsham Churchyard | 15 |
| Requiem | 16 |
| Faith | 17 |
| Beyond Noon | 18 |
| Poppy | 19 |
| Barmecide's Feast | 20 |
| Escape | 21 |
| Ferrari 410 SuperAmerica | 22 |
| On Such a Night as This | 24 |
| God Profound | 26 |
| Snow Expected from the North | 27 |
| Under The Same Blue Sky | 28 |
| Doors of Wood, Doors of Glass | 29 |
| Nocturne in a Minor Key | 30 |
| Whither goest Thou? | 32 |
| Symphony in J | 33 |
| Silent Cacophony for Two Voices | 38 |
| Undying Love | 40 |
| Alpha and Omega | 41 |
| Virtue's Light | 42 |
| Shadows of a Distant Heaven | 43 |
| Garwnant Forest | 44 |
| The Day of the Dead | 49 |
| Wild Flowers | 50 |
| Strange Street | 51 |
| All Hallow's Eve | 52 |
| Yes | 53 |
| Feeding the Kites at Gigrin Farm, Rhyader | 54 |
| Imaginary Me | 56 |

# Silent Places

A rutting, heaving track leads to this spot
imprinted with the crusty tread of
disturbed sleepers.
Warm, green larches leap
across the sun-filled slash of dust and
thirsty grass
their slender fingers touching.

The permanent-way was long since shown the
fallacy of permanence
and returned all to
the hare and the wild flowers and silence,
leaving smoke about the broad bridge-arch
to mark its passing.

Once, we leaned against the parapet
our fingers touching
from the bridge that now leads nowhere.
Our arms left no imprint
nothing marks our passing
only the crumbling masonry and the weeds.

Our sleep was disturbed; we awoke to see the
fallacy of permanence
and returned all to
the hare and wild flowers and the silence.

# Conversation Between the Wind and the Snow

For the wind was wicked
and the snow divine, and
the snow would shiver
and the wind would whine.

Whine and shiver,
rattle and howl,
Snow on the owl and wind on the river.

Blowing wind and falling snow,
What do they talk of? Where do they go?

But the snow just snittered and flittered
and fell
like a woman just flattered and
coaxed from her shell.

So cold, said the wind,
So rough, said the snow,
So clear was the moon
that the sky was aglow.

Darkness and moonlight,
The wind and the snow
Whistling through cracks
And settling below.

Settling on grass and houses and trees,
Moaning in chimneys
And freeze, freeze, freeze.

Jipperty - flipperty
Riddle-me-ree
Who can whistle?
Who can't you see?

I wish I could just be quiet
Shouted the wind.
I wish I was warm in bed
Sighed the snow.

Just to be quiet
And warm in bed,
Fingers on lips
And hands on your head.

Fiddle-de-dum
Fiddle-de-dee
You are the snow
And the wind is me.

Up in the atmosphere
Down on the ground
Windy-o, snowy-o
Round and round.

Let me gaze into my crystals
Snitters the snow.
Shall we shoot the breeze?
Wonders the wind.

Wanders the wind
Zing through the zither.
Silent the snow
Hither and thither.

Wily the wind
Sly the snow
Sneaking and peeking
Where none should go.

Whipping and howling
Weeping and growling
Flurrying and hurrying
Who knows where?

The wind is shaped
By the leaves and the trees
Swirling and shaking
The flakes and the breeze.

...and the wind chased the snow
and the snow played it cool,
but the wind kept on chasing
like a fool, fool, fool.

Cold-hearted snow,
Cold, cold heart,
Light-hearted wind
Doomed from the start.

If I wasn't snow
Then I'd be a river,
Said the snow to the wind
With a shudder and shiver

If I wasn't the wind
I'd be someone's breath,
Said the wind to the snow
Foreseeing his death.

Then a little girl breathed
And the wind did fade
And the snow hit the earth
Where it melted and laid.

For all conversation must come to an end
Like the wind and the snow
And the ebb and the flow
Each story will finish for all and for each
Like the move of the tide
On a stone-strewn beach.


Shiverdee, diverdee
Howlee-hoo
The snow it fell
And the wind it blew
Falling and blowing
Howling and snowing
Shiverdee, diverdee
Howlee-hoo.

Ice on the outer walls
Wind on the waterfalls
Ripple the water
Freeze the mortar.

Who can see the wind?
Who can smell the snow?
Nobody, nobody
That's how they go.

I am the snowfall
I am the wind blow
Snitter and whiz
That's how the world is.

# Diagnosis

Death glanced at me today
and I glanced back

I glimpsed it in the corridor.
It loitered amidst the throng
who stood around worrying,
waiting for their diagnoses.

I had spoken with the experts,
quiet, confiding,
and it seemed that I might survive
for now

Death looked me in the eye
across the crowded thoroughfare,
nodded slowly
and slouched off,
my future plans and dreams
hanging loose beneath its
vague limb

# Cold Air

There's menace about
a cold, early morning.
Things stored up, waiting.

A moment arrives,
standing between the door and
the cold air
when you want to turn back
but must go on.

An anxious hinge
that could swing this way
or that.

Cold air folds around you
like dread made flesh.
A door clicks shut and the air
draws you out, surrounds you
in a familiar ambush,
murdering you again
with another day.

# Edelman

Yes, I remember Edelman -
The name, because one morning
Of cold the cattle-trucks drew up at Radomsko
Unwontedly. It was early March.

The steam hissed. A guard coughed.
No one left and no one came
On the bleak platform. What I saw
Was Edelman - only this man

And two SS officers, those three only,
My thoughts bittersweet, of hopes high,
Some whit less now and Edelman afraid
His arms held up toward the sky.

And in that moment a Luger barked
Close by, and through him, bloodily,
Farther fell our hopes, all the Jews
Of Lodz and Warsaw.


(With acknowledgements to
Edward Thomas, 1878-1917)

# Memento Mori

A human skeleton,
bones yellowed by time
hangs in the entrance hall
of the Academy of Anatomy.

Students touch it for luck
as they laugh and pass by.
Professors too.
Children gaze at it, some intrigued,
some frightened.

Its empty sockets gape at the doors,
teeth grinning in a parody
of a smile.
It sees nothing and sees everything.

Those who rub the skull for luck
would recoil in shock if they could see
the person who once graced these bones
with her flesh.

*The crinolines, the lace,*
*the long, dark hair*
*and flashing eyes.*
*Passion and warmth*

*Promises and lies*

In the entrance hall
a door opens and
a light breeze stirs
the lattice
of bones.

A small plaque erected
years before
echoes her thoughts:

*Once, I was like you*
*One day, you will be like me*

# Shadows

Yesterday,
I had a minor accident.
Not surprising, given my age.

I slipped and fell
between the cracks
in my memory
into a vague place of shadows

It seemed as though there were
faces floating there
insubstantial, ethereal somehow,
there and yet long absent

I closed my eyes and
strained to catch a glimpse of
what drifted there

only faces, strangely,
illusions whom I had loved,
and loved still,
fleeting impressions from a vast,
endless archive

like mileposts drifting past
on some indeterminate journey,
taking me gently
on a slow, soundless shift

to become my own shadow
loved perhaps,
in someone's memory

# Topsham Churchyard

Here, the stones are laid flush
with manicured lawns
like an unwelcome hand of cards,
their souls rendered anonymous by winter rains

Move quickly now toward the steep flight
hurry down the steps
as they tip tap under your `
scurrying shoes

losing the churchyard's dead scent
hell-bent on living life in this world of senses,
like silent flotsam sweeping past
lost to sight in a mad swirl

The sun is warmer now
and the geese argue on the quayside
honking like ancient cars

the turning tide gathering momentum
causing anchored boats to sway,
lonely masts tinkling in the freshening breeze

somewhere across the broad estuary
the restless swell
tolls some hollow bells, echoing
the peals of laughter
from the carefree child
scattering the pigeons like wasted days

# Requiem

Click, clack; click, clack
goes the bolt
and a gleaming, deadly round
slides seamlessly
into the cold barrel.

...as the mist clears,
a ghostly figure emerges,
peering anxiously forward,
driven by his officers toward
the British lines.

Harry hefts the heavy Enfield
against his bruised shoulder,
aiming at the enemy's legs.

*I know that I don't really want to kill you,
nor you, me.*

Aim, allow for wind, squeeze -
a piercing *crack!*
a powerful recoil

...and for Heinrich Schmidt,
A plasterer from Lengefeld,
the war is over
with his life intact.

Feeling a ghastly, empty satisfaction,
Harry Patch reloads,
unaware of his long, life's journey
yet to come,
across this mad century.

# Faith

Beyond the whispering, lofty elms
the clouds pass, briskly white
in brilliant sunlight streaming
past the blue of angels' eyes.

Freshened air and breeze and
sky and beyond and beyond
and beyond, the lifted spirits soar,
placing perfection in a timeless truth -

*Praise Him*

# Beyond Noon

Through smeared sunshine glass
warm-laden bees float buzzing paths
across this drowsy day

Light-reflecting walls disport themselves
on distant haughty-houses
hanging silent on the aftermath of noon

Warm seabirds high on thermals
sing the sentient drowsing hours
gliding over the thick air

Cuckoo-clouds motionless
perch the overarching sky-blue
blanketing this warm world

Staring vacantly
into the reverberations
of a hot silence

# Poppy

Swept-sudden swan and flashing falcon-filmy
Rising, air-beat-feather, scatter-spiralling
Drop-flowered morn-dew on freshened-blustering breeze.
Wound-wincing earth has bled-bubbling at lark-song light,
Blood-poppy single-swimming in a flash-flood-green;
Slender slash-scarlet sets the fallow-field ablaze.

# Barmecide's Feast

And I, Schacabac,
poor, deluded wretch
staring from rain-puzzled panes,
throw a kiss to a hooded crow
cackling in drizzled branches.

Not a crow, not a branch
but a draggled priest
barking congregated shins

moonshine and mare's nests

Schacabac, staggering
from a glass of mulled air
intoxicated by air
bloated by famished plates
hey ho hey ho
wind must blow

Yes yes veil of tearful fears
I shall take you by the ears
Conform the shadow to the shape
Box the ears of those who gape

jig the antic Schacabac
jig to the frenzied feasted music
gabble the thousand babbled tales

and pass
uncomprehending
through the solid nothingness

# Escape

It left no footprints
No marks on the windows or doors.
All locks are intact.

I gaze at my hands, at my pen
and feel my pain.
It has gone, certainly,
leaving no immediate trace
only the fact of previous work.

It will return, they say
suddenly appear
*And you will forget that it ever went away*
as with the return of a prodigal son.

I dwelt in the sun for a while
but now my muse has flown
like some dark bat
which waits, dangling sinister from a branch
in my imagination's damp wood.

# Ferrari 410 SuperAmerica

*Rosso Red*
warm in the sun
*Carrozzeria - FARINA con volante*
*Nardi campanato*
Five gears with overdrive
Created in the lazy warmth of Modena
Imported Canada in fifty-nine.

Cameron Lake, Vancouver Island.
Hottest summer in a hundred years.
Miles to the nearest RCMP Detachment.
No problem.

Clear road.
*Power*

Rhythms of heat rising
from the scarlet metal hood.

One, two, three- *change up*- four,
*six thousand two hundred*
peak revs
hard bend
*down*, three,
forest, road
and lake expanse
*all that exists*

Leather hot on thighs
stripped to shorts.
Four point-nine vee-twelve
*responds instantly*
four, three, *bend left*
*foot down*, four,
*trees, water, endless road*

*Would that this were*
*eternity*

*Vancouver Island - 8th June 1981*

# On Such a Night as This

Standing alone astride this mountain
but one against the many,
the clear, full moon makes strange fictions
upon a man's mind.

Alone, in ghostly light
my imagination riots
like a press of common people
in a Roman market
and I, a centurion,
no more, no less.

*What madness brought us here?*

We set against a rain-crazed foe as
intransigent as Nubians.
Silures, a mad tribe who move at night
like shadows, killing us at random like foxes.

*The Gods sport with us*

This full moon is silent, soft its light,
clear the sky
and hushed the night.

Aurelius is a mighty man,
Tiber-deep his thoughts:
*Why fret when all before and all
to come, shall be borne away
in the eternal flow?*

I shall die here,
my carcass rotting in this ground
to leech a nourishment to these
heathen trees, this violent grass.

And this sovereign sphere,
cold goddess of Stygian night
will light my trodden earth to some Valhalla
wherein, as ghostly shade,
I shall meander mountains such as these
and guard this moonlit flank of Rome

*on such a night as this*

# God Profound

I know that God exists
and this I know

That in the sparkle of a wash of water
pebble-flashed in tumbling streams
or in the weightless presence of an airy bird
darting-eyed on a balanced branch

or in the background-blue of cloudless skies
viewed from chaotic carpets of forest floors

and in the damp, wooded breeze
which draws me, reverential, into towering pines
claiming me, my heart and soul

This is where, all around

God profound

God is found

# Snow Expected from the North

In the churchyard, the earth is warmth
sprouting life

sap oozes.

sightless headstones suck on the dead air

gusts of wind plunge
into pools of uneasy crows
scattering their wings like veils

In the next room
a figure slumped in a final chair
thinks into the mirror of the yew tree
listening to the sounds of her hollowed feelings
beating in her hallowed heart

*It seemed that as she had lived*
*she had slept*
*Awakened for just a moment*
*and all her life was gone*

Snow is expected soon, from the north.

# Under The Same Blue Sky

A female police officer,
middle-aged, flustered, overweight,
stands at this dusty junction
in busy Brooklyn,
packing a large Beretta
on her swollen hips.

She cannot give us directions
to Brooklyn Heights.
She has never heard of the place
apparently.

We take a sunny hike and
ask a broken-down old man
the same question.
He surprises us with clear, summarised
directions and we reach
the beautiful streets
of tree-lined Brooklyn Heights,
bathed in February sunshine.

Maybe he should have been
the police officer
and she the derelict,
wandering the confused streets unarmed
by knowledge,
while he, heavily-armed with professionalism
and a gun, dispenses assistance
to a grateful public.

But nobody ever said that
life was fair - neither he
*nor* she - presumably.

# Doors of Wood, Doors of Glass

Weighing nothing, whispering through
an absence of light,
an owl has opportunity to reflect.

The wings are failing, falling, but the world
draws no closer, stays far below,
remaining visible in some other world, as a door hewn from
oak
seen through glass.

No limbed finial to unlatch this door, to step inside,
only feathers. An exhausting enigma this flight,
a disordered phalanx of
questions.

*Wondering how other birds pass through
effortlessly.*

Being an owl is being nothing.

Flashing by, always baffled by this strange physics,
wormhole

which, when night is day, opens

inwardly.

# Nocturne in a Minor Key

I.
In the high room the spider spins.

We sit you and I in silence.

In the garden, the children laugh and play
their future is another day
so we say

A line of slender trees stands like a wide brush
painting white onto a grey horizon.

Towards the evening the rooks head home
and flittermice assemble
flitter, flutter
like the veils on a dancer.

Towards the evening urgency increases
Time is getting short

We must wake
for Life might be taking us
where we have
no wish to go

such sad inheritance creating nothing
out of a dead life

II.
On the salt marsh the shrike
shrieks its piercing thoughts
shrouded in a mist of its uncertainties

Held in space, in time
meandering the daylight's
pointless paths


III.
A silent clock marks ticking pixels
on a static screen.
The clock does not tick
not yet.

Explain and dissemble
they serve the same master

such intrusion this intrusion
noisome dross and noise
bringing stultifying rain
swirling through the mind's
dark drains

*O, desert of waters*

IV. .
In the branches of a skeletal tree
swathed in iridescence
a weary angel clothed in sadness
weeps myriad tears into a
misty marsh

weeps for the gathering darkness

*salt in the sea*

Time is getting short

# Whither goest Thou?

Whither goest thou, dear brother? The heavens have opened wide,
The dog has rent your only hat - you're sure to catch your death.
The fields are lank and soaking and the tracks have turned to mud,
And you're always wont to tell me that you cannot catch your
breath.

*Sooner the raindrops patter on my world-worn head*
*Than patter on the earth o'er my grave when I'm dead.*

I'll heed thee not, dear sister, I needs must grasp the day,
I've wasted too much precious time in hiding from the rain.
There's many shapeless in their graves would fain be live and wet
And linger freshly-breathing in the damp, green fields again.

*Let the raindrops patter on my world-worn head*
*They'll patter soon enough on my grave when I'm dead.*

Pluvius, pour out your heart, your flood of life on me!
I wipe the raindrops from my eyes with many a tear of joy,
Casting mind back long ago to when I wandered wild
And wet and cold and happy, for then was but a boy.

*Let me feel once more the cooling rain upon my old grey head*
*The cold raindrops will patter soon upon my earthen bed.*

# Symphony in J

## 1st Movement

The soul is a lonely cathedral
*Drownd in the floode*

Luther on the steps;
*Hier stehe ich; ich kann nicht anders*

I said to the lilies consider, consider.
Standing on the Sea of Tranquility
Near the shore of the Bay of Storms,
Bleeding, I raised my thumb
And obliterated the sins of the world.

*For where is the angel who stands upon the sea?*
*And where his little book?*

Nothing is stable in this dusty sea
Neither the rock that cannot move
Nor the wind which never gusts
Weightless footprints
Floating in a sinless sand.

*Mallow, mayweed, heartsease and flag*

Cankerous dry stone wall
Upright and alone too long
Falls faintly to the bosom of the nodding field
Warm smiling in fiendish suns
    embers dancing in a lifeless fire
    the virginity of death.

## 2nd Movement

Gardeners in the Paradise of the World
Strip your souls;
Draw on, naked darkness
Night of the senses
While these, our greatest strengths
Strongest virtues
shrivel
abandoned

Not yet have we lived, not yet
For the darkest prince pursues
the awful philosophies
theologies of misery

       Fabulators of a tangled web
lie about us,
dark, dank earth absorbing their moistures,
redefining, renewing them, returning them
as spring-tides of bitter wine
washing at the feet of tongueless trees

*the centurion's gift*

       On mushroomed magic hill
       The wizard in his scholar's cell looks down
       from rose-hipped windows of polished ivory
       Pauses
       and pencils lines.

## 3rd Movement

Lilies gape where once two paths entwined
beneath an elm magnificent
      baptised in light

August
and the marigolds melt to dust

Moon and mayfly
     .........................................
Deep space unsquares immediate reality
dispersed to timeless voids
accelerated into blind
inscapes
of history
evanescent yet amaranthine
fabric Gordian-wove

      fables resounding in silence

..... and green cathedrals pressing
ancient vaulted roots leeching
grasping gold-heaped depths

worms turn
slowly in their leaf-greened mould

this soil is turmoil and confusion
tumultuous pulsing fusion of a billion spores

....... and the grave-sapper ploughing
dank, carrion-sky-compassed
inhumed gravels

weary light-cloudy mackerel days
splashing slowly into dusk
trickling heartbreaks of horizon

## 4th Movement

Let us drink the vineyard and
eat the olive bough
            which we did not plant
embody testimony
            which we did not write

            Look linger back
            O God of the Gates
            harbouring hateless forms
            you, with drifting bullock cart and
            clouds.

The bee and the lizard
are not one
Nor the white dove nor
terracotta tile

            illusive parameters hold the mind in
            plagiarism of the self
            No logic in the case;
            *The world is what the case is.*
....................................................................................
Beyond this wicked sunlight and the sky
concealed within a coop of sightless sound
the jester floats
            and smiling,
            gently steers

*Peccavimus*

The soul is a lonely cathedral
trapped on icy steppes of
solitary night

the lonely wolf
praising Mozart and the stars

Sysyphus toiling like an ant.

# Silent Cacophony for Two Voices

Eleven years from my mother's womb,
the boles dropped from my sapling tree
urged on by the fluid motion of my springtime.

I met him then, that other,
that presence, that rainbowed voice,
voicing his views
viewing his effects
as I acquiesced and shrivelled.

All of youth's life passed me by.
Everything that mattered.
Gone.

Later, on our tiresome journey together,
his work complete,
he gradually fell behind like a dropped hem
and later still drew ahead
a thoroughbred surging on the bridle,
but no longer were we together.

Either slinking behind or striding before
he remains,
an apparition
neither to side nor
to side
looking straight ahead.

He has led me by the nose,
whispering his advices,
led me never to believe in myself
like a spiteful brother
calling from a dim doorway,
hissing in a swirling fog
*a cage in search of a bird*
yet he was me
is me
but walks now
without my being.

I glance back briefly at the chaotic road behind,
where throngs of painful facts gather,
a waving, mocking crowd of disorderlies
and, turning wearily forward, see
the road before me, moving fast towards a close horizon
lying to the west

I am caught up in the mainspring of time
which has slowly unravelled and will stop,
leaving silence and a few precious jewels
under the scattered stars.

Let me live now.

# Undying Love

Thou swore undying love, such cannot last;
As mother curses babe at pain of birth,
Swift words not truly meant and quickly past-
So weasels quickly flash and slip to earth.
All things which breathe the air are root in death,
Thus murmured nothings thence to nought return;
Once-willing flesh unwilling parts with breath,
Frail words which scented air, in air shall burn.
No matter, mistress fair, no matter sweet
Relinquished love - exist no tears, love's darts,
But only leaves; shades born of brown which meet
And melt into the soil where lie our hearts.
Where sang the nightingale in tend'rest night,
Now hordes of blacken'd crows erupt in flight.

# Alpha and Omega

Night moves, and Hecate her scattered flock
Star-shepherds to her fold each twinkling ray,
Wanes silent in the air as slumb'ring cock
Awakes from sister-death and cries the day.
Up, up then sun, thou hot and beaming liar,
That half this globe might view Parhelion's flight,
Nought-knowing of the mumm'ry in thy fire
Nor sensing yet the stealth-returning night.
The fresh'ning air that balmy blows, alas
Falls colder when false Helios doth slope
Behind horizon's cowardly arras
And gives the lie to brightness and to hope.
Emerges dark the alpha of our breath,
And darkness cloaks the omega of death.

# Virtue's Light

Thy maiden blush sweet-holds this eye and yet
Delights which enter here on light depend;
Is then thy beam the seed that doth beget
Such beauty and doth formless dark amend?
If this be so, then twilight's adumbrage
Is but a practised gesture from a scene,
As players mouth their words across a stage,
Which tell of things which hath in truth not been,
Nor shall they but within their writer's mind.
So nought hath I to fear from sun's demise,
Though all the orbs of heaven be rendered blind,
And darkness falls across these mortal eyes.
No matter that I dwell 'midst blackest night,
This mind thy form shall trace in virtue's light.

# Shadows of a Distant Heaven

Windows of a failing heart.
Blue irises
faded.
*Eyes of a forgotten god*

Pupils dilated by the effort
of their learning
leaning together before the blackboard
dusty of discontent.
Voided by weary dusters
of discarded feeling.

*The eyes have it*

Love's butterfly cringing under
the analyst's pitiless gaze.

Time yet breathes
while its mirror
Life
floats silently on deceptive streams
Muffling its oars to pass unnoticed
Gliding over gentle hills

*Shadows of a distant heaven*

This terminal patient impatient
for release
Eyeing the convulsive graph
drawing each impulse from a
                              fading dream

Craving the thoughtlessness
of a simple green line
crying its shrill final note
for a still heart

# Garwnant Forest

## Spring

Awake, to a soaring rhapsody
of sovereign pines
the rippled cold of a secluded lake
and the ridged horizon of a hill

tread slowly
where the brambled berries
breathe through the cool air
braced by the high breezes

Oak moth and leaf miner
horseflies and horses
trekking the tracks,
hooves in the mud floor

a flurry of undergrowth as a
rabbit breaks cover and
scurries into the green
beyond

fritillaries
mad among the violets
yellow heat across the floors
of fringed forest

*all life in a leaf*

dead needles pin the living shoots
under the ground
parting around
the swollen thrusts
of new life

from somewhere in the deep wood
a staccato chatter
sends eerie echoes
of ancient conflicts
tearing like bullets
through the long leaves

the ordered drill of the woodpecker
breaks the ethereal silence
deep in the timbered thicket
hammering out his hollow message of
territorial ambition
the rapid rainbowed head
tracing its urgent bursts
in a tight arc

silence returns


## Summer

here, the heat is silent
in this noisy light
limping through the air
like a dead cloak

there, a shimmering, shy unicorn
glimpsed in a glade
*a trick of the light*
*in this otherworld*

a sense that everything
is alive
and flourishing
under the sun

shy in deep seclusion
shrouded safe from prying eyes
and busy highway racing
across these high, watered hills.

Soaring above the sheltering canopy
of wet and tangled woods
a red kite
wheels and turns
far from its dishevelled nest
roaming restlessly
sharp eyes scanning
hanging silent on sublime wings
plunging in a sudden dive
of gifted violence

warily
a lonely fox flits
through the forest
paws pitter-pattering
like rain


## Autumn

...and the birch leaves drift down
to the soil's pulse,
falling from the branches
in a final, flashy encore.

the season's swaying ocean of colours,
evocations of earth, of lemons
and emeralds,
sparkle on the dappled roof
while shades of forest light
invoke the cooling season
*silence*

Only the high breezes
whispering through the ragged raiments
of creaking, roughnecked giants
rooted in their mad march
across the leagues of virgin hills

while miles above,
high across the wind-strewn forest
of tall skies,
a glinting insect crawls its
dawdling way toward
the rain-swelled seas

weakening sunlight
drifts down on cooling
wefts of woven spinney
deferring to the cold
illuminance
of the shivering moon's
late harvest

*darkness*

beneath this tilted earth
the weasel softly shrieks
his mad capers
echoing the ghostly antics
of the moon's shadow

...and what little warmth remained
is gone
drawn towards the cool stars

...then clouds drift across the cold moon
sending streaks of fresh rain dancing
down through the lonely dark

lonely, dark

...sleep now, for morning creeps
across a distant horizon
bringing winter days


## Winter

Trees loom through a chilling haze
a silent shroud of freezing fog
suspended in an atmosphere
of censorious silence

Shapes seem to float in an
eerie, shrinking light
as the world's thoughts
turn inwards

Colder now, in the palace
of the Ice Forest
as its tiny creatures
nuzzle closer in their
snowy quarters,
sleeping their way to Spring.

A bitter wind
flurries the snow
drifting into every crevice

and as the day melts away
into the sleeping forest
nothing remains
but snow
and the cold stars scattered
like a river of diamonds
across a dark heaven.

# The Day of the Dead

Smooth-circled bell's internal
concave crown-reflection clapping
thunder-sullen
booming over Popocatepetl
muffled under rain-gorged drooping clouds.

Applause placating unseen gods
fragmented in the valley-vast of tears.

Evening rains descend
mixing mud and man
cloud and cantina
rolling thunder in the vast bell.

*bellwether*

All despondent trail its wake
none may avoid the music of the bells.
Neither blind nor deaf
nor dead - in them this day belongs.

These their severed sightless tongues lapping
soft bell-bellies
tolling thunder in the dark-soaked air

# Wild Flowers

Alone, we ponder
In the potting shed of our mistakes.
Among shrivelled stems
deep within musty peat
eloquently dormant,
sleep all the answers to
every fumbling question never asked.

Shaking foolishness from rubber boots,
wiping condensations of misunderstanding
from our spectacles,
fresh possibilities occur
like brightly-coloured packs of seeds.

Trees take an age to grow
and should only be transplanted while they're young,
in case they fail.

Wild flowers are the strongest of the lot,
resisting outside influences.
Without benefit of peat or potting shed,
*wild flowers survive*

# Strange Street

It seemed as though the
hypnotist had snapped his fingers.
Walking awake, I awoke
suddenly,
finding myself in a strange street
in which were only shadows.

A voice would whisper this, another this,
and this.

The questions were grey and dark
and long past.
*But why?* and *Why not?*
Asked aloud and
*If only you had...*

*For pity's sake!* I called out.
Grey shadows turned, glanced
and glided on.

On, where the world goes
in search of something
or someone.

*So many chances,* a voice whispered.
*Come,* echoed the grey breeze.

And so it was and is
from the waking dream
where the shadows glide
and the heart cries out
cries from the heart

*I always loved you*

# All Hallow's Eve

All Hallow's, winter midnight of the year,
Dark eve, when harried souls beseech thy prayer,
Believe, and let thy voice conjoin the throng,
The host of kneeling voices praising God.
O throng, whose haunting notes soul's fevers share;
O soul, dark secret, truth's clear light lays bare.
This dark and dreadful midnight of the soul,
When lambs, abandoned, lost and freezing lie,
And wind's chill fingers pluck at mem'ry's harp,
Behold, sin's doleful music of regret.
Its notes abound, are moaning, pleading Thy
Forgiveness, sweet redemption ere they die.
When I, O Lord, am thrown upon this night,
Pray God forgive me, pity thou my plight.

# Yes

Feel beyond a blunted bridge
Soft beneath the stunted stalk
A curtained pulse

About the bowels the fires play
Dancing in the solid seams

Here the fleshy tubing titters
Flitters, flickers and flares
Belly yes

In a sealed, in a closed
In a safe, safe, safe
What the colours of a tree are
What the tiny tunnel says
In the dark

Eye lit, underarm, up back straight
See the pretty voice
Gasp the purple promise-may
Breathe the inner drum, drum, drum

Against decide, create one fall
Flushed with flowing fantasy
Beyond the bonding arching bridge
Sail-soul fairaway
*Euphoric*

# Feeding the Kites at Gigrin Farm, Rhyader

Cold winter skies
over Gigrin Farm

dozens of flustered crows
cackle around in the skittering wind
waiting as the hands on the farmhouse clock
toil towards two

A scattering of red kites swirls
on the high gusts
watchful on wind-blustered wings
loitering above the blooded field

the old, polished clock
chimes the hour
in the silent, ticking farmhouse

seventy pounds of fresh, crimson meat
scatters in pieces
across the feeding ground
like the aftermath of some gruesome battle

slowly, in ones and twos,
the sturdy, jet-black crows plop down
and strut about the carnage
pecking at particular cuts

a melee of crows and kites
swirls in the air
keening and squawking
a bewildering confusion of birds

then one huge kite, then another
and another
swoop down in crazy vertical dives
snatching bloody helpings
from the hectic ground

on and on it goes
as the grisly arena
is stripped of evidence

and only then do the blood-streaked suspects
lift into the air in a ragged retreat
from their bestial work
amidst the flesh-strewn field

# Imaginary Me

I read a poem once
about a young woman who had
an imaginary boyfriend
who was a lot less bother than
the real thing.

This led me to thinking
about my own situation and
I began to wonder what
it would be like to have
an entirely imaginary life.

Why bother with reality
when everything in the world
was there for the taking?

I began to imagine my happy teenage years
and how well I had done at school.
Then I imagined all the girls I'd been with
and the amazing career that I'd carved.

What fun life was!
I had never known such happiness
and personal fulfillment.
Why had I ever bothered with real life at all?

Later, relaxing on the sun deck of
my villa overlooking the bay at Monte Carlo,
I suddenly thought about my *real* life
and all the people whom I loved.

I summoned my maid who, as you might guess,
was the current Miss France,
and told her to pack my things as I had
to leave for home immediately.

*But I couldn't find my way back.*

I now seem to have been involved in some
medical emergency, because I find myself
strapped to a hospital gurney in a completely
white room.

I hear voices, some of them familiar,
and, although horizontal and immobile,
I am still able to travel around from place to place,
speaking to various fascinating people, none of whom
seem able to understand me.

I am no longer certain whether any of this
is real or imaginary, the lines seem to have become blurred.
You are looking at me, I think.
Do I know you from somewhere?